T0014498

STUFF
EVERY
MAN
SHOULD
KNOW

Library of Congress Cataloging in Publication Number: 2020921572

ISBN: 978-1-68369-272-0

Printed in China

Typeset in Sentinel & Gotham

Designed by Ryan Hayes
Illustrations by Vic Kulihin
Production management by John J. McGurk

10 9 8 7 6 5 4 3 2

Quirk Books
215 Church Street
Philadelphia, PA 19106
www.quirkbooks.com

STUFF EVERY MAN SHOULD KNOW

BRETT COHEN

QUIRK BOOKS
PHILADELPHIA

To Randi, Ilivia, and Sawyer, who inspire me to be a better man

_____

INTRODUCTION

Guys, I'm going to let you in on a little secret. Our learning doesn't stop when our formal school education ends. After all, life's a journey, not a destination. And that journey is going to present every man with a variety of situations. Some you'll be prepared for, and some you won't. But each instance will broaden your experiences, expand your mind, and shape your character.

So prepare yourself for a lifetime of learning—a lifetime of making yourself a better man. Some of this you will pick up naturally along the way. Some of it will require an investment of time and resources. And some of it you'll find right here in this book.

As I set out to revise this book (originally published in 2009), I brought with me a new set of life experiences and lessons I've learned in my own journey. This revision still includes the timeless, traditional skills you might expect. But it's also peppered with more timely advice for today's man. Some of the entries are essential information, while others are just for fun—because, after all, we should enjoy the ride.

I acknowledge that my journey isn't the same as every man's. So in addition to drawing on my first-hand knowledge, I have researched these topics and incorporated expert advice to create a book for all types of men.

As you navigate this book, and your life in general, my hope is that you will open your mind to new ideas, open your heart to all different types of people, and open yourself to new experiences. Because, in doing that, you will truly make yourself a better man.

Now sit back, relax, and pay attention. This stuff is important.

DOMESTIC
LIFE

HOW TO MAKE YOUR BED

Whether you sleep alone or share your bed with a partner, you should get in the habit of making your bed every morning. It makes the room look neater and the bed more inviting when you're ready to slip back into it at the end of the day. Sure, you can just pull the blanket over the whole bed. But with a little practice and minimal extra effort, you can actually make it properly.

- **Clear the bed.** Remove all pillows, blankets, and top sheets from the bed. If you are making the bed for the day, you can leave the fitted sheet on the bed. Otherwise, . . .

- **Replace the fitted sheet**. If you are making the bed after washing all your sheets, place the fitted sheet over the mattress. Lift the corners of the mattress to tuck the elasticized corners of the sheet underneath. Continue to tightly tuck the sheet around the entire mattress so that there are no wrinkles in the sheet.

- **Drape the top sheet.** Place the top sheet over the fitted sheet with the larger hem near the top of the bed where your pillow goes. Align it evenly with the head of the mattress. If your top sheet has a pattern, lay the pattern facedown so that when you fold the top of the sheet down, the pattern will be visible. Make sure the top sheet hangs evenly on both sides of the bed.

- **Tuck the top sheet.** Start by tucking the sheet under the mattress at the foot of the bed. Tuck it neatly so that it's smooth. Then pull the sheet tightly on one side of the bed and tuck that side under the mattress. Once again, ensure that it's smooth to create a crisp corner. Repeat on the other side of the bed.

- **Spread the comforter.** Lay your blanket, duvet, or comforter over the top sheet. Make sure that it is spread evenly across the bed, with an equal amount hanging on both sides. The top edge of the comforter should be about 6–8 inches below the end of the top sheet.

- **Fold the top sheet.** Take the edge of the top sheet and fold it down over the comforter. If the sheet has a pattern, you should now see the pattern clearly.

- **Place pillows and accessories.** Fluff your pillows and place them at the head of the bed. Arrange decorative pillows, if any, in an upright position against your pillows.

> **Tip:** You should wash and change your sheets every 1-2 weeks.

TOOLBOX ESSENTIALS

Though you may never be called upon for a big construction project, things break and need to be fixed. When projects pop up, you'll want to be prepared. Here's the bare minimum of what every guy should have in his toolbox.

- A tape measure
- Carpenter's level
- Claw hammer
- A stud finder
- Flat-head and Philips-head screwdrivers
- Nails and screws of varying sizes
- A monkey wrench or wrench set
- Allen wrenches
- A set of pliers (including slip-joint pliers with toothed jaws)
- A handsaw
- Utility knife with retractable blade
- A pair of work gloves
- Spray can of WD-40
- Duct tape and/or electrical tape
- Safety goggles
- Variable-speed reversible drill
- A staple gun with $1/2$-inch staples
- Sandpaper
- Superglue, wood glue, and tacky glue
- A flashlight

TIPS:

- Every tool you buy is a long-term investment. A good hammer should last a lifetime. Buy from a retailer you can trust, and invest in quality products.

- Add a small notebook to your toolbox and use it to record important data about your home. Keep a record of various paint colors so you can match them in the future. Note the last time you changed the batteries in your smoke detectors. List the specs of any unusual light bulbs used throughout your home. With a little research, you might be able to find a good app or website that will help you track all these items.

HOW TO HANG A PICTURE FRAME

The art of hanging the picture should be as skilled as the art inside the frame.

1. Select the location. Don't hang one small picture on a large wall. Try to hang the frame so that it extends or matches the lines of furniture or windows (i.e., a long frame above a long sofa). Make certain that there is plenty of room for the frame.

2. Hold the frame up to the spot where it will be hung and mark the top with a pencil. The frame should be placed so that the middle is at eye level.

3. Select an appropriate hook. A nail-and-hook is fine for smaller frames. But if you're hanging a larger frame, be sure you are nailing directly into a wall stud (use a stud finder to locate one). Or buy some hollow-wall anchors, which grip the drywall more securely and distribute the picture's weight.

4. Measure the space from the top of the frame to the hanging mechanism. If it is a wire, make sure you pull the wire taut before measuring.

5. Measure down that same distance from your original pencil mark on the wall. Make a new marking.

6. Nail or drill your hook into that new marking.

7. Hang and straighten the frame.

HOW TO
JUMP-START A CAR

A dead battery is an easy thing to fix—provided that you've got a set of jumper cables in the trunk. (You do have jumper cables in your trunk, right?)

1. Refer to your car's owner's manual. It may provide important information on the particulars of your specific car. Some models require you to use special lugs designed for jump-starting, instead of connecting directly to the battery.

2. Recruit a driver with a working automobile. Park the working automobile beside your car so that the two batteries are as close as possible. Be sure the two cars are not touching each other.

3. Put both cars in park with the emergency brake engaged. Turn the cars off and remove the keys.

4. Pop the hoods of both cars.

5. Attach the red-handled (positive) clamp at one end of the jumper cable to the positive terminal on the dead battery.

6. Attach the red-handled (positive) jumper cable clamp at the other end to the positive terminal on the fully charged battery.

7. Attach the black-handled (negative) clamp at the first end of the jumper cable to the negative terminal on the charged battery.

8. Ground the remaining black-handled (negative) jumper cable clamp to an exposed piece of clean metal on the dead car's engine—usually a nice shiny bolt will do the trick.

9. Start the working automobile, and allow it to run for 2 to 3 minutes.

10. Start the car with the dead battery. If the engine starts, wait 3 or 4 minutes, and then remove the clamps one at a time in reverse order. Allow the "jumped" car to run for at least 30 minutes before turning it off, to ensure that the battery is fully charged.

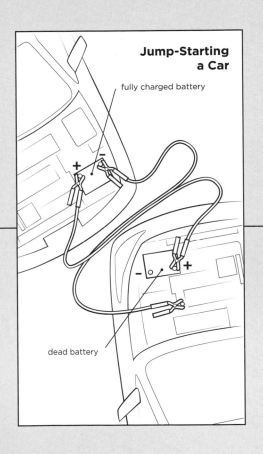

Jump-Starting a Car

fully charged battery

dead battery

HOW TO CHANGE A FLAT TIRE

Sure, you can call roadside assistance. But in the hour you wait for the tow truck to arrive, you can probably change the tire yourself and be back on the road.

1. Drive to a safe, flat, dry area. Driving on a flat tire may damage your car, so do not prolong the trip longer than necessary. Pull over as soon as possible, and be certain you are all the way off the road.

> **Tip:** Some vehicles have "run flat tires" that will allow you to drive at a reduced speed until you can get home or to the repair shop

2. Set the car in park and engage the emergency brake. Place a large rock or piece of wood in front of and behind the tire opposite the flat to prevent the car from rolling.

3. Locate your spare tire and jack. In many vehicles, these will be hidden underneath the upholstery in the trunk. Note that many modern vehicles now include a "donut" instead of a full-size spare; this miniature tire is designed to get you only to the nearest service station. It should not be used for extended traveling.

4. Remove the hubcap and loosen—but do not remove—the lug nuts with a four-way wrench.

5. Place the jack under the car. Consult the owner's manual for the proper placement of the jack. Never place the jack under any material that looks like it might bend, crumple, or collapse.

6. Use the jack to raise the car.

7. Remove the lug nuts and the tire.

8. Place the new tire on the mating surface. Replace the lugs and tighten them by hand.

9. Spin the tire a few times to make sure it turns properly.

10. Use the jack to lower the car to the ground, and then remove the jack.

11. Tighten the lugs using the four-way wrench.

THE ONLY KNOT YOU'LL EVER NEED TO KNOW

How dependable is the bowline knot? Consider that the Federal Aviation Administration recommends its use when tying down light aircraft. And if it's good enough for securing a Cessna, you better believe it'll keep your canoe from drifting away. The bowline knot is so simple, even children can tie it. In fact, they often learn by using this basic mnemonic:

1. **This is the rabbit hole.** Make a loop in your rope.

2. **Out comes the rabbit.** Pull one end of the rope through the loop.

3. **It runs around the tree.** Wrap the end you pulled through the loop around the other end.

4. **And hops back into the hole.** Pull it back through the loop, and tighten the knot.

The Bowline Knot

This is the rabbit hole.

Out comes the rabbit.

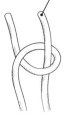

It runs around the tree.

And hops back into the hole.

KITCHEN ESSENTIALS

Although you may not be gunning for a spot on *Top Chef*, you do have to eat. Here's a list of must-have items to stock in your kitchen. The quantities may vary depending on how often you plan to have guests and how interested you are in cooking elaborate meals for them. But this is a great place to start.

- **Tableware:** a set of flatware (forks, knives, and spoons), a set of steak knives, a set of salad plates, a set of dinner plates, a set of soup bowls

- **Glassware:** a set of 6 water glasses, a set of 6 wine glasses, a set of 6 cocktail glasses, a set of 6 coffee mugs, a set of 6 pint glasses

- **Serveware:** 1–2 large serving platters, 1–2 large serving bowls, serving utensils, a water pitcher, a coffee pot, a wine carafe or decanter

- **Cooking tools:** a can opener, measuring cups, measuring spoons, a liquid measuring cup, a cutting board, tongs, a spatula, a slotted spoon, a wooden spoon, a whisk, a set of stainless-steel mixing bowls, a mesh strainer, grilling tools, a pizza cutter, an ice cream scooper, a knife set (usually includes an 8-inch chef's knife, an 8-inch bread knife, a 6-inch utility knife, and a 3½-inch paring knife)

- **Cookware:** a saucepan, a large pot, a nonstick frying pan, baking sheets

- **Food storage:** reusable storage containers, zip-top plastic bags, aluminum foil

- **Appliances:** a toaster, a blender, a coffee maker

HOW TO MAKE THE PERFECT OMELET

Every man should have a signature breakfast dish, whether you are cooking for a date that stays the night, your partner on your anniversary, or your parents when they're in town. Omelets are impressive and easy to make. The following recipe makes 1 omelet.

1. Crack two eggs in a bowl. Add a splash of milk and a sprinkle of black pepper. Mix with a fork until smooth.

2. Coat a small pan with cooking spray or butter and place over a medium flame. Let the pan heat for a few moments.

3. Pour in the egg mixture so that it evenly fills the pan. Let it set for 30 seconds.

4. Use a spatula to lift the edges of the egg mixture so that the uncooked eggs can move to the bottom.

5. Once the egg mixture is almost cooked, add some fillings to one half of the pan. Fillings can include diced tomatoes, ham, bacon, spinach, broccoli, mushrooms, smoked salmon, onions, chives, spices, sauces, and virtually anything else you'd like to include (see suggestions, opposite). The only requirement, typically, is some kind of shredded cheese. Do not overfill.

6. Use a spatula to fold the empty half of the egg mixture onto the filling; the result will have the shape of a half-moon.

7. Let the omelet cook for another 30 seconds.

8. Slide your spatula under the omelet and transport it to a plate.

CLASSIC OMELET FILLINGS

Alaskan omelet: salmon, sour cream, chopped tarragon

Denver omelet: ham, green peppers, onion, cheddar cheese

French/Western omelet: ham, tomatoes, mushrooms

Greek omelet: spinach, black olives, feta cheese

Hawaiian omelet: ham, pineapple chunks, cheddar cheese, Monterey Jack cheese

Irish omelet: mashed potato, lemon juice, chives

Polish omelet: potatoes, onion, zucchini

Seafood omelet: crab meat, shrimp, onions, mushrooms, sour cream, Swiss cheese

Southwest omelet: ham, tomato, green peppers or chilies, onions, salsa

Spanish omelet: sliced potato, onions, red and green peppers

TIPS FOR THE GRILL

Learning to cook is an important skill. The grill is a great place to start. Make the most of your grilling with these simple tips.

- **Chicken:** Marinate chicken overnight to allow the flavor to sink in. Also, white meat cooks faster than dark meat, so plan your timing accordingly.

- **Steak:** When steak is finished cooking, remove it from the grill and let it sit for a few minutes to allow the juices to redistribute through the steak.

- **Burgers:** Flip your burgers only once. This will give them great char marks and keep the juices sealed inside.

- **Fish:** Use a fish basket to keep the fish from sticking to the grill. It will also prevent the top layer from flaking off and releasing some of the flavor.

- **Ribs:** Reduce your grill time by boiling ribs ahead of time.

PERSONAL
APPEARANCE

FIFTEEN WARDROBE ESSENTIALS

With these items in your closet, you'll be prepared for virtually any fashion situation.

1. **Shoes.** Of all your measurements, your shoe size will remain the most constant over the course of your life. Find a quality pair of black leather loafers and make the investment.

2. **A suit**. If you purchase just one, choose a classic dark suit that will lend itself to a variety of events. Spend a few extra bucks to have the suit properly tailored.

3. **A tuxedo.** At some point, probably in your twenties or thirties, you'll likely have a string of weddings to attend. If your crew leans toward the formal side and will opt for black-tie affairs, you should purchase a classic two-button tuxedo with notch lapels. This look never goes out of style. In the long run, it's cheaper to own than to rent.

4. **Dress shirts.** A white shirt is a safe and classic option. Supplement with other colors and patterns that complement your personal style. Dry-clean your dress shirts without starch and have them pressed by hand. They will look crisper and last longer.

5. **Belts.** Your belt color should match your shoes. Black with black. Brown with brown.

6. **Socks.** These are a subtle, understated means for expressing your personality. Choose from solids, stripes, argyle, or polka dots, to name just a few of the available patterns.

7. **Ties.** Like socks, your tie can say a lot about your personality. Purchase at least one new tie every year to keep up with trends.

8. **Blue jeans.** Darker jeans look more formal and work well for a variety of social situations. No rips, no fraying—unless, of course, these are intentional style details.

9. **Khaki pants.** A darker color allows you to transition from the office to a night on the town without changing clothes.

10. **T-shirts.** A white T-shirt paired with jeans or khakis makes for a nice, classic, casual look. Supplement your wardrobe with three or four V-necks and rounded-collar T-shirts of various colors.

11. **Collared shirts.** A polo shirt is a classic and versatile look. It can be layered under a sports jacket or worn with jeans.

12. **Sweaters.** Sweaters are good for layering over a collared shirt in the winter or as a standalone item in the spring. A charcoal gray V-neck goes well with a suit, jeans, or pants.

13. **Underwear.** Choose from boxers, briefs, or bikini briefs, based on your own comfort. Keep a few in mint condition for special occasions.

14. **Sneakers.** You need two pairs: one for the gym, and one for a stylish night out.

15. **Accessories.** Sunglasses, watches, cuff links, hats, pocket squares, scarves, and other accent items are great ways to incorporate your personal style into even a basic wardrobe. Have fun with your look, and occasionally step out of your comfort zone.

DRESS CODE CHEAT SHEET

Is there a difference between black-tie optional and semiformal? Surprisingly, yes.

White tie: black tailcoat with silk facings and a white shirt, collar, waistcoat, and bow tie

Black tie: tuxedo

Black-tie optional: tuxedo or formal suit

Semiformal: formal suit or sports jacket with a tie and trousers

Business: formal suit or sports jacket with a tie and trousers

Business casual: trousers and a dress shirt

Casual: jeans; the type of shirt depends on the attendees

HOW TO SEW ON A BUTTON

Why should a guy know how to sew on a button? Because it's cheaper than buying a new shirt.

1. Select a button and thread that match the article of clothing. Thread that is slightly darker than the fabric is ideal, because the stitches will blend better (lighter thread stands out more).

2. Thread a needle so that there is 1 foot (30 cm) of thread on both sides of the needle. If you have trouble, lick the end of the thread before inserting it through the needle's eye.

3. Knot the two ends of the thread together.

4. Position the button on the fabric, making sure that it is aligned with the corresponding buttonhole as well as the other buttons on the garment.

5. Starting from the underside of the fabric, push the needle through the fabric and one hole of the button. Pull the thread all the way through.

6. Push the needle down through the next hole in the button and through the fabric, pulling the thread all the way through.

7. Bring the needle back through the fabric and a hole in the button, and repeat this process about ten times to ensure that the button will stay put (Figure A).

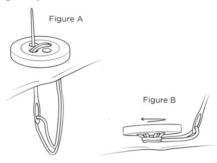

Figure A

Figure B

8. Then pull the needle and thread through the fabric under the button, but not through a hole. Pull the thread all the way through. Wrap it around the thread that holds the button to the fabric three or four times (Figure B).

9. Push the needle back through to the underside of the fabric and pull it taut. Angling the needle almost flat against the fabric, push it through the fabric but not to the surface (Figure C).

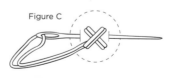

Figure C

10. Before you pull the thread taut, pull the needle through the loop in the thread a few times to create a knot. Repeat several times, overlaying stitches to secure the knot (Figure D).

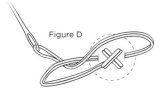

Figure D

11. Trim excess thread.

> **Tip:** Place a penny under the edge of the button while you sew to ensure there is enough slack for the button to be pulled through its corresponding buttonhole and accommodate the additional layer of fabric.

HOW TO TIE A TIE

In today's business-casual world, ties are increasingly less common—but there will always be weddings, funerals, and graduation ceremonies. With a basic four-in-hand knot, you'll always be prepared.

1. Lift your collar.

2. Wrap the tie around your neck under the collar, with the wide end on the right side. The wide end should lie twice as long as the narrow end.

3. Cross the wide end over the narrow end and back underneath twice (Figures A, B, and C).

4. On the second pass, instead of wrapping back around, push the wide end through the loop made near your neck (Figure D).

5. Pass the wide end through the knot near your neck (Figure E).

6. Keep the wide end on top of the narrow end as you pull it through.

7. Tighten by drawing the knot toward your neck while holding the narrow end with your other hand.

8. Straighten. The tie should hang to your belt buckle with the top lying longer than the bottom (Figure F). If that doesn't happen, untie, adjust the ends accordingly, and try again.

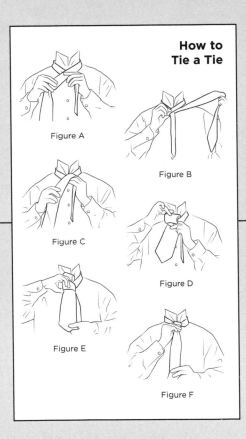

How to Tie a Tie

Figure A

Figure B

Figure C

Figure D

Figure E

Figure F

HOW TO SHAVE PROPERLY

In a world full of high-tech electric shavers with free-floating pulsonic blades and whisper-silent pop-up trimmers, does anyone really need to know how to shave with a plain old razor blade? The answer will seem obvious when you arrive in Houston for the big account meeting—but your luggage is rerouted to Cleveland. All you need to save the day is a can of shaving cream and one very sharp piece of metal.

1. Wash your face with soap and water. To soften your skin, wet a washcloth with warm water and hold it to your face for 30 seconds. This will ensure a much smoother shave.

2. Using a shaving brush or your hand, apply the shaving cream over the area you wish to shave. If you don't have shaving cream, hair conditioner makes a good emergency substitute.

3. Be sure to use a new (or relatively new) razor blade. Dragging a dull piece of metal across your face is a surefire way to sabotage your appearance.

4. Starting on one side of your face, shave from the top of the beard line down to your jawline in one even stroke. Move with the grain of the hair. Be sure to hold the razor at a 45-degree angle or less to reduce nicks and cuts. Rinse the razor between strokes and continue with the rest of your face in the same manner.

5. Starting on one side of your neck, shave from the hairline on your neck up to your jawline in one even stroke. Continue with the rest of your chin/neck in the same manner. You may want to pull your skin taut with your free hand to ensure a closer shave.

6. Rinse the shaving cream from your face and look for spots you have missed. Pay careful attention to the areas around your mouth, nostrils, and sideburns.

7. Soothe nicks and cuts by splashing your face with cold water; it will often cease the flow of blood. If you are prone to shaving injuries, invest in a styptic pencil, which constricts the blood vessels around an open cut.

8. Upon completion, pat your face with a clean towel and apply a moisturizer to prevent your skin from drying out.

> **Tip:** A straight razor offers the closest shave possible, but using one is extremely dangerous. Shaving with a straight razor requires tremendous patience and practice—which may be in short supply at six thirty in the morning, when you're racing to catch your train. If you'd like to experience this classic shave, ask a trained professional—your barber—to do it.

HOW TO MAINTAIN FACIAL HAIR

Facial hair can come in a variety of shapes, looks, and lengths. No matter what style you prefer, you'll want to maintain a regimen that keeps your facial hair healthy, clean, and looking good.

- **Be patient**. Once you've made the decision to grow a beard, you'll need to give it some time to develop. It's recommended that you don't trim it for the first 4–6 weeks while it fills out (the exact time will depend on how quickly your hair grows and whether your desired look is more Zach Galifinakis or ZZ Top). Cut stray hairs as they pop up and perform a regular maintenance routine while the beard is growing and after you've reached peak length.

> **Tip:** If you struggle with growing a full beard because of some sparse areas, it's best to keep your beard trimmed on the shorter side.

- **Wash it regularly.** Trapped food and flaky skin cells can cause itchiness. Scrub your facial hair a few times per week with a specialized beard cleanser. After washing, gently pat your beard dry with a towel to avoid frizz or split ends.

- **Pamper your beard.** Routinely apply a beard oil and a conditioning cream to keep the hair healthy.

These products will hydrate and soften the whiskers while also preventing dry skin beneath the beard.

- **Brush your beard.** Purchase a beard brush and use it daily. Brushing distributes the natural and applied oils throughout your beard and exfoliates your skin underneath. This step is especially important if your beard is long.

- **Select a style.** Once the hair has filled out, you can trim your beard to the style that best suits you. Seek the advice of a hairstylist if you are unsure. But, generally speaking, it's recommended that you match your beard to the shape of your face.

   Oval: Most beard styles will work with this symmetrical shape.

   Round: Keep the sides short and let the beard grow fuller below your chin to help elongate your face.

   Oblong: Keep the bottom short with fuller sides to add width to a narrow face.

   Square: Let the beard grow fuller below your chin, and style it into a rounded shape as it becomes longer.

   Triangular: If you have a wide jaw and a narrow forehead, keep your beard short and close to your face.

Diamond: If you have wide cheeks and a narrow forehead and jaw, keep the sides short and grow a fuller beard below the chin.

- **Trim your beard.** Whether you are trimming to define a style or to maintain your current shape, you'll need the right tools. A beard comb, facial hair scissors, and an electric beard trimmer with guard heads will cover most maintenance needs. Always trim your beard when it's dry. If you aren't sure what length you want, start with a guard head on the higher side and work down. Comb the beard to shake out loose hairs and use the scissors to snip away stray hairs.

TIPS FOR DEALING WITH HAIR LOSS

As a man, there's a good chance you will face thinning hair or balding in your lifetime. In most cases, it's genetic and there's little you can do about it. While this realization can be emotionally taxing, the best thing you can do is accept it—if not embrace it—and remember that your self-worth isn't tied to the hair on your head. As you move toward acceptance, here are some things to consider.

- **Try a new hairstyle.** Speak to your hairstylist or barber about the best way to wear your hair. Typically, shorter styles work better for thinning hair. But if you have a bald spot, an expert can suggest ways to accentuate your thicker areas to maintain a fuller style.

- **Try a new look.** New glasses, facial hair, or body piercings will move attention away from your thinning hair. Not only will it give other people something different to focus on, it may also give you something new to feel good about. (For tips on growing facial hair, see page 42.)

- **Own it.** Buzz your hair short or shave it off completely. While this change may feel extreme, it puts the power in your hands as opposed to watching Father Time slowly steal your hair away.

- **Speak to your doctor.** If your hair loss is sudden and persistent, speak with your healthcare provider or specifically a dermatologist to get to the root of the problem. There are a range of factors that can cause hair loss. And in some cases, you can slow or reverse the effects just by changing your diet, your vitamin intake or even your hair-care routine.

Accepting hair loss can be hard. Those feelings are totally valid. If you're struggling with this change, consider the following options to regrow hair or mitigate the loss.

- **Try medication.** There are over-the-counter and prescription medications available that help regrow hair or stop the balding process. Typically, those medications work with daily use and the effects will reverse once you stop using them. Your doctor can advise if such a treatment is right for you.

- **Consider transplants.** This process relocates hair from the back and side of your head to the top. It's expensive and may need to be done repeatedly while you continue to lose your hair.

HEALTH
AND
WELLNESS

TIPS FOR MAINTAINING A HEALTHY DIET

The food you eat directly impacts your energy levels, muscle efficiency, weight, mood, and overall health. It's necessary to indulge yourself every now and then, but here's how to develop and maintain generally healthy eating habits.

- **Seek balance and variety.** To ensure you get the right nutrients to power your body, eat a mix of all the food groups (vegetables, fruits, grains, proteins, dairy products, and oils) while minimizing sugary foods, sodium, and saturated fats.

- **Be heart-healthy.** Make sure to include omega-3 fatty acids, which are present in salmon and tuna. Minimize fatty meats like bacon and sausage, which are high in sodium and saturated fats that have been linked to heart disease.

- **Embrace fiber.** Consuming fiber as part of whole, unprocessed foods is critical to keeping your digestive system clear and healthy, which in turn will keep you feeling well. Generally, fruits, dark-colored vegetables, and whole grain breads are good sources of fiber.

- **Eat your veggies.** And berries. And nuts and seeds. In addition to key vitamins and minerals, these foods are packed with antioxidants, which protect your body from breakdown and disease.

- **Drink water.** The average man should drink 64–100 ounces of water per day. You'll need more if you exercise. But, ultimately, you can trust your thirst. If you find it hard to remember to hydrate, it's helpful to keep a water bottle with you at all times. Try setting smaller goals, such as reaching certain intake targets on an hourly basis, or look for apps that remind you to drink periodically throughout the day. If you struggle with the taste of water, try adding a lemon or lime slice for extra flavor.

- **Do not skip meals.** Set a regular mealtime schedule and try to eat every 4–5 hours to keep your system fueled and prevent hunger from pushing you to make a bad decision.

- **Keep healthy snacks on hand.** If you tend to get hungry between meals, keep healthy snacks close at hand. When almonds, carrot sticks, or an apple are within reach, you may avoid grabbing the more convenient, and maybe less filling, junk food snacks.

- **Speak to your doctor.** Ask your doctor about your ideal weight, target daily calorie intake, foods to avoid, and supplements to take, if necessary. You should also discuss whether your current medical conditions and medications will be impacted by a dietary change.

- **Consider working with a registered dietician** to develop healthy eating habits that will last a lifetime.

WHEN TO SEE A DOCTOR

It's important for all men to seek preventative care. The chart below offers general guidelines for healthy males; because research is always changing, check with your doctor for the most up-to-date recommendations. Family and personal medical history could require you to visit more regularly or start seeing a specialist at a younger age. Overall, it's a good habit to end each visit by asking the doctor when you should schedule your next appointment. And of course, chronic or new issues may require more frequent visits.

WHAT	WHO	HOW OFTEN
Routine physical, blood work and shots	Physician	Ages 19–21: once every 2–3 years Ages 22–64: once every 1–2 years Ages 65+: once every year
Dental cleaning	Dentist	Once every 6–12 months
Body skin exam	Dermatologist	Once every year

Eye exam	Optometrist	Once every 1–2 years
Colonoscopy	Gastroenterologist	Ages 40+ (or younger if there's a family history of colon cancer): once every 10 years
Prostate cancer screening	Urologist	Ages 50+ (or younger if there's a family history of prostate cancer): once every year

EXERCISE TIPS

Exercise is essential for keeping your body in shape and maintaining your physical health as you age. It can also be fun, improve your mental health, and be a great way to connect with new people. Here are a few key things to consider when maintaining an exercise routine.

- **Choose an exercise regimen that best suits you.** The key is to get your body moving. If you want to make it a social activity, consider team sports or a group exercise class. If you want something convenient that can be done anywhere, try running. If you want to be indoors, get on a treadmill. If you want to focus on a specific area of your body, try weight training. You'll be more motivated if the exercise excites you.

- **Stretch regularly.** Gentle stretching will improve your flexibility, help your body move more efficiently, and relax your muscles. And it may reduce your risk of injury. Everyone's different—some people like to stretch before working out, others after—so experiment to find what works best for you. Give priority to your hamstrings, lower back and shoulders. You can create a basic morning stretch routine at home or attend a yoga or Pilates class.

- **Do it right.** Make certain you are performing the specific activity in the proper way. You may want to work with a trainer, coach, or more experienced friend to assist you in creating a program and showing you how to do it correctly. Also, resist the urge to overexert yourself; instead, start slow and with lower weights or lower levels of activity.

- **Take a break.** Give yourself a moment of rest between exercises. Use the time to rehydrate. Also, give yourself a rest day every few days to allow your body to recover.

- **Mix it up.** While it's good to get into a workout routine, it's also good to try new things to keep you engaged or mix in a variety of activities to work different muscle groups. If you are hesitant to try a new activity, ask a friend to join you.

- **Think holistically.** It's important to balance exercise with other parts of a wellness plan, including a healthy diet, solid water intake, good sleep habits, and proper mental health care.

HOW TO PERFORM A PROPER PUSH-UP

Before you drop and give me twenty, learn how to do push-ups properly—and most effectively.

1. Lie chest down on the floor. Place your palms flat on the floor, shoulder width apart. (Increasing this distance will make the push-ups easier; decreasing it will make them harder.) Your chin and the balls of your feet should be touching the floor. Breathe in.

2. Straighten your arms as you exhale and push your body away from the floor. Your palms should stay in the same position. Your legs should stay pressed together. Your body should form a straight line from head to heel.

3. Pause when your arms are at full extension.

4. Bend your arms as you inhale and lower yourself to the ground. Touch your chest and knees to the floor. Repeat.

A Proper Push-Up

straight line from head to heel

balls of feet on floor

palms flat on floor

Note: You should aim to perform at least 20 push-ups in one minute.

HOW TO PERFORM ABDOMINAL CRUNCHES

Forget about old-fashioned sit-ups; most experts now recognize that they're hard on your back and an inefficient form of exercise. If you really want to hone a six-pack, try doing some abdominal crunches instead.

1. Lie on your back with your feet flat on the floor. You will work more efficiently (and comfortably) on a mat or carpet. Bend your knees so they form an inverted V. Have a partner secure your feet to the floor. The distance between your feet should be as wide as your hips. Place your hands behind your head; your elbows should be pointing out.

2. Curl up so that your head, neck, and shoulder blades leave the floor. Do not allow your arms to push you up; instead, leave the heavy lifting to your abdominal muscles. If you're doing it right, you'll feel it.

3. Pause and then lower yourself to a starting position. Repeat.

A Proper Crunch

elbows pointing out

leave heavy lifting
to abdominal muscles

keep feet hip width apart

Note: You should aim to perform at least 40 abdominal crunches in one minute.

HOW TO PERFORM A PROPER PULL-UP

Combine this exercise with push-ups and abdominal crunches, and you'll have one hell of an upper body.

1. Stand under a pull-up bar. If you don't have gym equipment handy, you can use the limb of a tree.

2. Grab the bar using a pronated (overhand) grip. If you require assistance reaching the bar, use a step-stool or chair that you can later kick away.

3. Let your body hang for a moment. Relax your shoulders and try not to arch your back.

4. Pull your chest toward the bar by bending your arms in a single smooth movement. Keep your torso straight without jerking your muscles or flailing your legs.

5. Raise your body until your chin reaches the bar. Pause for a moment, then lower yourself back down. Repeat.

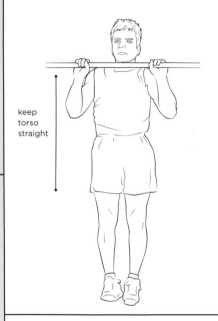

A Proper Pull-Up

keep
torso
straight

Note: Some men lack the upper-body strength to complete even a single pull-up. If you can complete 15 of these in a minute, we salute you.

HOW TO START A SIMPLE SKINCARE ROUTINE

Fun fact: Your skin is your largest organ. And it's the one that's most exposed to the effects of the outside world. Follow this simple routine to protect your skin while keeping your face looking clean and healthy.

1. Wash your face once or twice daily. Do this to remove all the dirt on your face. A normal bar of soap will dry your skin out, causing it to create more oils. So, opt for a gentle, hydrating soap specifically designed for use on your face. Wash your face in the morning when you wake up, as your pillow is a hotbed for bacteria. Cleanse again prior to going to bed if you have oily skin.

2. Exfoliate once per week. After you wash your face, use a gentle face scrub to clear away any dead skin, open your pores, and bring the healthier skin cells to the surface.

3. Moisturize your skin. Once you've cleaned your face and removed all the dirt, bacteria, and dead skin cells, you'll want to rehydrate and protect your face. A moisturizer will deliver vitamins and nutrients to the skin while also hydrating and preventing it from creating excess oil. Apply the moisturizer to a dry face once or twice daily after washing and/or exfoliating.

4. Protect yourself from the sun. Apply sunscreen with SPF 30 when you will be outside for extended periods. It will block harmful UV rays that lead to sunspots, wrinkles, sunburns, moles, and cancer. Often, the SPF is built into a moisturizer that can perform double duty.

Note: If you have dry or oily skin, adult acne or other skin conditions, you should speak to a dermatologist, who can provide individualized skincare treatment.

HOW TO RELAX AFTER WORK

Relaxation is essentially the absence of stress. Because stress can impact your physical and mental health in a multitude of ways, it's important to know how to manage it. Since relaxation is unlikely to happen *during* work, here are some tips for how to unwind *after* work.

- **Don't feel guilty about it.** Relaxing doesn't mean you are being lazy. It may feel unnatural to choose to do something for yourself or do nothing at all. But taking time for yourself is important to recharging your body and spirit.

- **Leave work at work.** The very nature of work is stressful and contradictory to relaxation. If you can, leave your documents and computer at the office, turn off email notifications, and note in your group calendar that you're unavailable after a certain time. This may not be practical if you are self-employed, work from home, or don't work a typical 9-to-5 schedule; whatever your situation, try to set realistic boundaries in order to create as much separation as possible.

- **Create time for relaxation.** This could mean scheduling it on the calendar or completing your after-work obligations upon arriving home to free up the rest of your evening. Either way, avoid over-committing in order to make time for yourself.

- **Maximize your time to unwind.** You may not be able to allocate several hours each day to relaxation, but even smaller pockets of time can be effective. For example, taking 10 minutes to yourself when you get home will help your mind and body transition away from work. You can even designate your commute home as some quality "me time" by listening to a soothing playlist or reading a book on the bus or train.

- **Create a relaxation ritual.** This could be as simple as washing your hands and changing your clothes when you get home. Or it could be more elaborate, involving meditation and breathing exercises. Find what works for you, and over time, the habit will train your body to acknowledge that this is the time to decompress.

- **Create a space for relaxation.** Roommates, kids, and partners may make it difficult for your home to be a relaxing space. If you can't allocate a full room, you can designate a space that allows you to pursue certain endeavors. For example, if painting relaxes you, set up an easel near a window.

- **Seek out activities that help you relax.** Take a walk. Go to the gym. Practice meditation. Get a massage. Join a yoga group. Take up a hobby. Play a board game. Read a book. Meet up with friends. Chill on the sofa and watch TV. You get the idea. It's all fair game if it helps you relax.

HOW TO GET INVOLVED IN A MEANINGFUL CAUSE

This entry may feel out of place in the Health and Wellness chapter. But volunteering to make the world a better place can help you meet new people, learn new skills, reduce stress, provide a sense of purpose, and even make you feel happier and healthier. Here's how to start.

1. **Make a list of what matters to you.** Think about the issues you are passionate about and the types of changes you want to see in your world. Your world can be defined in any way you want. It can be local, such as your town. It can be specific to a certain population. Or it can encompass larger issues that effect a broad region or multiple communities.

2. **Choose one thing that matters to you most**. Your time and resources are limited, and you can't fix every problem that exists. Choose one that feels extremely meaningful to you. It's likely that several of your issues are interconnected, but starting with one issue can provide you with a way to make meaningful change.

3. **Seek out people or organizations that share your beliefs.** Meaningful impact takes time and is likely to be achieved incrementally over a longer period through the collaborative work of individuals in support of larger organizations. Network locally to find others that share your passion

Speak with or write to politicians that share your values. Contact organizations that are dedicated to doing the work you care about.

4. **Contribute your time, energy, *and* money.** There are a number of ways to get involved, and to maximize your resources, you can pursue more than one, such as volunteering with one organization and donating money or goods to another.

> **Volunteer.** Contact the organization and inquire about volunteer opportunities. Ask questions about the organization's mission to ensure it aligns with your values. Ask questions about the time commitment and any required training to make sure it fits your availability. Also, consider your skill set and what specific expertise you can offer the organization. For example, if you are a web developer, you can help update their website.

> **Donate.** Set aside a portion of your paycheck for contributions, or donate monthly if you can to support the mission year-round. If it's important for you to see your contribution in action, seek out local organizations that you can meet with about your donation.

Spread the word. Use your excitement and passion to get others involved. Organize a fundraiser that introduces the organization to your friends or a volunteer day that encourages your coworkers to join in. If it's a national organization, perhaps there's a local fundraising event that you can get involved with or start on your own.

5. **Enjoy yourself.** The best experiences benefit you and the organization. If you find yourself no longer interested, reassess the situation and your involvement. The opportunity may no longer be a good fit for where you are in your life. Or maybe something has changed within the organization that no longer motivates you.

HOW TO GET A GOOD NIGHT'S SLEEP

Restful sleep is essential for recharging your body and setting you up for a successful day. If you have trouble getting enough shut-eye, consider these suggestions.

- **Create a daily sleep schedule.** Get in the habit of going to sleep and waking at the same time. This will create a sleep/wake cycle for your body, and with time, you may train yourself to wake without an alarm clock. Waking naturally may also make you feel more rested and ready for the day.

- **Consider your environment.** Find a room temperature that works for your body. Eliminate distractions like lights and noises. Tidy up your bedroom if the mess adds stress (and remember to make your bed; see page 14 for more). Employ a sound machine if background noise helps you doze off.

- **Manage your daily lighting.** Sunlight or bright light can increase your energy during the day while also improving your sleep quality at night. On the other hand, exposure to intense lighting at night tricks your brain into thinking it's daytime and reduces your melatonin level, which helps your body relax. So increase bright light exposure during the day, and decrease blue light exposure in the evening by putting your phone and other electronic devices away well before bedtime.

- **Be mindful of caffeine, sugar, and alcohol.**
  Elevated levels of caffeine stimulate your nervous system and prevent your body from relaxing. Because caffeine can stay in your blood for up to 8 hours, minimizing or eliminating consumption after noon can contribute to better sleep. Sugary foods should also be avoided in the evening for similar reasons. Additionally, alcohol is known to disrupt sleep by altering melatonin production.

- **Develop a bedtime relaxation routine.** Do something that clears your mind and helps your body relax. Take a hot bath or a shower. Listen to calming music. Meditate. Read a book. Try different things to find what works best for you.

- **Know how to fall back asleep.** It's normal to wake up in the middle of the night. If you have trouble falling back asleep, try to avoid stressing about it. Instead, take slow deep breaths, or practice progressive muscle relaxation techniques, in which you tense and relax each muscle in your body one at a time. These will help you relax your body without overstimulating your brain.

- **Consult a doctor.** If you have trouble sleeping, you should speak to a doctor to rule out a sleep disorder. Additionally, your doctor may recommend over-the-counter supplements such as melatonin or prescribe something stronger to help you sleep.

ETIQUETTE
AND
SOCIALIZING

HOW TO MAKE FRIENDS AS AN ADULT

When we're younger, school practically forces us to socialize and make friends. As we get older, we get busier. We get more set in our ways. We have less time to socialize. So we get more selective in how we spend our free time and who we want to spend it with. Whether you are settling into a new city, a new job, a new phase in life, or maybe you just want a clean slate with a new group of friends, here are some tips for meeting people in adulthood.

- **Look around.** You may already have casual relationships that can turn into a deeper friendship. Perhaps there are people at your office. Or maybe there are other parents at your child's school. Maybe you are on a text group where you don't necessarily know everyone. Consider what you already know about these people and determine if you want to get to know them better.

- **Take a class.** Part of friendship is having shared interests. Consider your passions and hobbies, and seek out opportunities to meet people that share them. Join a cooking class. Participate in a weekly tennis lesson. Inserting yourself in an existing group that shares a common purpose removes some of the initial pressure to carry a conversation. And if you don't find friendship there, at least you learned something new.

- **Be a joiner.** In addition to paid classes, there are lots of free opportunities to meet people with shared interests. Take your dog to the dog park. Join a book club through your local library. Volunteer at an organization you are passionate about. Once again, you'll have an immediate shared interest and can expand the relationship from there.

- **Turn to social media.** Facebook is great to keep up to date with current and old friends. But perhaps there's someone you follow and admire on Twitter, Instagram, or another social network. Reach out via DM and strike up a casual conversation. Additionally, there are apps and websites that can help you meet new people. Join a group, follow local pages, and attend in-person meet-ups.

- **Take it to the next level.** Once you identify someone with whom you'd like to create a more meaningful friendship, start with a casual offer. Suggest something as a natural extension to the situation you're in, like grabbing lunch during work or a drink after the cooking lesson. If you already have their contact info, try engaging in a text conversation around your shared interests and expand from there.

- **Make it stick.** All relationships require some effort to get started and continue to grow. Make the time to get together. Share information about yourself. Listen to them and internalize what they are saying. Check in regularly—even if it's via text.

HOW TO CHECK IN WITH YOUR FRIENDS

Checking in on your friends shows you are there for them. Not only is it helpful for maintaining and deepening your relationship, it also opens the door for them to share something they may be struggling with and need support or advice with. While there's no one-size-fits-all-friendships approach, here are some ways you can check in on friends.

- **Send a text message.** Texting may be casual, but for many people, it's the preferred method of communication. It can also lay the groundwork for a follow-up conversation. A quick note wishing your friend good luck on a critical project or just saying hi lets them know you are thinking about them. It also opens the door for them to respond in whatever way they need.

- **Listen.** If your friend needs to vent, listen. If your friend needs to share their struggles, listen—even if you can't identify with what they're going through. Validate what they are saying to show you understand. Sometimes, offering your ear is more valuable than offering advice.

- **Give advice if it's warranted.** Ask if your friend wants your advice (they may not!). Admit to the level of advice you are qualified or not qualified to give. And accept the fact that your friend may have already tried that approach and it didn't work, or maybe they just don't want to follow your advice. Don't push. Don't get argumentative. There may be more background to the issue than your friend wants to share.

- **Offer your services or resources.** If your friend is struggling, identify the ways you can meaningfully help. Picking up groceries or cooking them dinner are things we can all do and might take some of the burden off your friend. Offer to go on a walk with them to help clear their mind. Don't pretend to be a psychiatrist. If you sense that your friend is having deeper mental or physical struggles, point them to a place where they can get professional help.

- **Continue to be there.** Checking in may boost your friend for the moment, but making concrete plans for the next hangout shows you're there to support them in the long term.

THE PERFECT TIP FOR EVERY OCCASION

WHO	HOW MUCH
Airport valet	$1 per bag
Barber/Hairdresser	10–15 percent
Bartender	$1 per drink
Car wash employees	$2–$3 for basic wipe down
Coat check/valet	$1–$2 per coat
Concierge	$5
Doorman	$1 per bag
Food delivery	10 percent
Furniture delivery and movers	$10 per person

NOTES

Consider adding an extra dollar or two if the bags are particularly heavy or cumbersome, or if the weather is inclement.

If you see the same barber regularly, consider giving him a holiday tip equal to the cost of one haircut.

Consider $2 or more if you plan to sit at the bar all night. 15% of the bill for larger orders.

$5–$10 for more complicated services like vacuuming, waxing, and other add-ons.

Most coat-check personnel are paid less than minimum wage and depend upon tips.

Up to $20 for exceptional service.

For hailing cabs, helping with packages, etc.

$2 minimum.

You may choose to increase this amount if the delivery requires special handling or assembly.

WHO	HOW MUCH
Golf caddie	$3 per bag
Hotel bellhop	$1–$2 per bag
Hotel housekeeping	$2–$5 per night
Parking valet	$2
Room service	$5 minimum
Server	20 percent
Shoe shiner	$2
Taxi driver	15–20 percent of the fare
Uber/Lyft driver	$1–$2 for shorter rides

NOTES

10–20 percent if he actually caddies your round.

Add a dollar or two if he shows you the room. Minimum of $5.

Depends on the quality of the hotel and service.

Up to $5 for exceptional service.

If gratuity is added to the check, you don't need to tip.

Consider a larger tip if your party is six or more or if you received exceptional service. In Europe, gratuity is often included in your bill.

Add a few dollars if he gives you a hot stock tip.

If you pay by credit card, remember that the cabbie is charged the card-handling fee.

Tip extra for traffic, longer distances, and if the driver helps with baggage.

HOW TO OPEN A BEER BOTTLE WITHOUT AN OPENER

Sooner or later, you're bound to find yourself with a perfectly good six-pack—and no way to open the bottles. Fear not: everything you need is right at hand.

1. Grab another beer bottle.

2. Place the bottle you wish to open in your non-dominant hand. Hold that bottle at its neck in the upright position. Hold the second bottle horizontally by the label.

3. Fit the shallow ridge found at midcap of the opener bottle under the bottom edge of the other bottle's cap. Using the opener bottle for leverage, press up and pry off the other cap.

4. The goal is to pry the cap away from the bottle. There are a variety of other items that can accomplish this task, including a screwdriver, envelope opener, knife, belt buckle, lighter, and table top.

How to Open a Beer Bottle Without an Opener

opener bottle

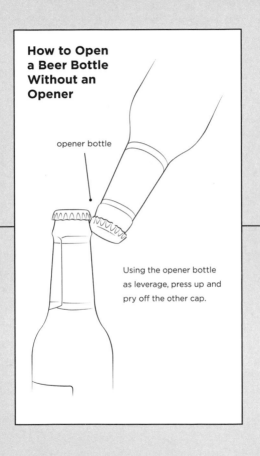

Using the opener bottle as leverage, press up and pry off the other cap.

ELEMENTS OF A BASIC BAR

You never know when a party is going to break out. Be prepared for any type of occasion with the elements of a basic bar.

UTENSILS

- A jigger measure
- A glass or plastic stirring rod
- A cocktail shaker with a good lid
- An ice bucket with tongs
- A corkscrew
- A bottle/can opener

GLASSWARE (RECOMMENDED 4–6 OF EACH)

- Cocktail or martini glasses
- White-wine glasses
- Red-wine glasses
- Champagne glasses
- Snifters
- Pint or pilsner glasses
- Highball glasses
- Rocks glasses
- Shot glasses

WINE AND SPIRITS

- 1 liter of vodka

- 1 liter of dry vermouth
- 1 liter of gin
- 1 liter of bourbon
- 1 liter of whiskey
- 1 liter of rum
- 1 liter of Scotch whiskey
- 1 liter of triple sec
- 1 liter of tequila
- 1 bottle of white wine
- 1 bottle of red wine
- 12 bottles of beer

MIXERS

- 1 bottle of grenadine
- 1 bottle of cola
- 1 bottle of club soda
- 1 bottle of tonic water
- Assorted juices (orange, grapefruit, cranberry, lime, and tomato)
- Hot sauce
- Plenty of ice

GARNISHES

- Green olives
- Cocktail onions

- Maraschino cherries
- Lemon
- Lime
- Apple
- Orange or grapefruit
- Carrot and celery sticks
- Sugar, salt, and pepper

DRINKS THAT CHANGE YOUR BREATH . . .

. . . FOR THE BETTER:

- Gin and tonic
- Gimlet
- Vodka and cranberry
- Any drink with citrus

. . . FOR THE WORSE:

- Beer
- Any sweet drink
- Any drink with milk
- Any drink with chocolate

Tip: If you have any doubt about the freshness of your breath, ask the bartender to prepare two mojitos for you and your companion. These popular rum-based cocktails are served with an abundance of fresh mint. Chewing the leaves (and even the stems) will eliminate any trace of halitosis.

FOUR COCKTAILS TO IMPRESS YOUR DATE

In order to impress, do your research. Find out what liquor your date prefers and mix accordingly.

- **Bourbon:** Whiskey Sour

In a cocktail shaker, combine 2 ounces of bourbon, $3/4$ ounce of fresh lemon juice, and $3/4$ ounce of simple syrup with ice. Shake for 20 seconds and strain into a rocks glass with ice. Garnish with an orange wheel and a Maraschino cherry.

- **Gin:** Negroni

In a mixing glass, combine 1 ounce of gin, 1 ounce of Campari, and 1 ounce of sweet vermouth with ice. Stir until well chilled. Strain into a rocks glass with large ice cubes. Garnish with an orange peel.

- **Tequila:** Tequila Sunrise

In a highball glass, combine $1^1/2$ ounces of tequila and $3/4$ cup of orange juice with ice. Slowly pour in $3/4$ ounce of grenadine, drizzling it down the side of the glass so it settles at the bottom. Garnish with an orange slice and a Maraschino cherry.

- **Vodka:** Cape Codder

In a highball glass, combine 2 ounces of vodka and 4 ounces of cranberry juice with ice. Squeeze the juice from $1/2$ lime into the drink. Garnish with a lime wedge.

TWO COCKTAILS FOR YOUR PARENTS

Show your parents that you have matured past college by mixing up a gin martini.

- **Gin Martini:**

In a cocktail shaker, combine $1^2/_3$ ounces of gin and $^2/_3$ ounce of dry vermouth with ice. Shake and strain into an iced martini glass. Serve with an olive.

And if your father doesn't like gin, don't worry. Make the old man a vodka gimlet instead.

- **Vodka Gimlet:**

In a cocktail shaker, combine $1^1/_2$ ounces of vodka, 1 ounce of lime juice, and 1 teaspoon of powdered sugar with ice. Shake and strain into a martini glass.

TWO COCKTAILS FOR A PARTY

Mixing up big-batch beverages saves you from playing bartender all night. Here are two suggestions that will allow you to enjoy the party, too.

- **Classic Margarita:** Serves 8

In a large pitcher, combine 2 cups of tequila, 1 cup of triple sec, 3/4 cup of fresh lime juice, 3/4 cup of sweetened lime juice, and 3 cups of ice. Stir. Pour 2 tablespoons of kosher salt on a plate. Rub the rim of each glass with a lime wedge. Dip the rim of each glass into the salt. Pour the margarita mixture into each glass.

- **Moscow Mule:** Serves 8

In a large punch bowl, combine 4 cups of ginger beer, 3 cups of vodka, 1 cup of freshly squeezed lime juice, 1 cup of fresh mint leaves, 2 sliced limes, and 4 cups of ice. Stir. Garnish copper mugs or glasses with mint and ladle the punch into the mugs.

HOW TO ORDER A BOTTLE OF WINE

Ordering a bottle of wine can be intimidating, especially if you don't know the proper etiquette. Here are a few tips on selecting a wine and instructions for participating in the tasting ritual.

1. Consider what you will be eating with the wine. Reds typically complement heavier meals, such as meat and pasta. Whites pair better with lighter meals, such as chicken, fish, and salads. If you want to really show off, try pairing your cuisine with a wine from the same region of the world.

2. Select a wine from the menu that meets your price range. A more expensive bottle doesn't necessarily translate into a better-tasting bottle.

3. When in doubt, ask the server or sommelier for advice. Be sure to mention the type of wine you are looking for and your approximate budget. There's no need to mention dollar amounts. Simply point to a wine on the menu and say, "This is what I would ordinarily order, but I'm interested in something different this evening. What can you recommend?"

Once you have made your selection, the server will bring the wine to your table and begin the tasting ritual.

1. The server will present the bottle with the label facing out. Confirm that it is the bottle you ordered.

2. After opening the bottle, the server will present you with the cork. Inspect the cork to ensure that it is not damaged, cracked, or dried out. Do not smell it.

3. The server will then pour a small amount of wine into your glass. Swirl it to release the aroma: Grasp the stem of the glass and, keeping the base firmly on the table, move the glass in small circles.

4. Bring the glass to your nose to smell the bouquet. Confirm that it doesn't smell rancid or musty.

5. Taste the wine. Confirm its flavor and indicate that the server may pour the rest of the glasses. If anything about the bottle is unsatisfactory, express your concerns immediately. A good server will handle the situation without making you uncomfortable. Choose another bottle or ask the server to recommend a personal favorite.

FACTS AND NOTES ABOUT WINE

MOST COMMON RED GRAPE TYPES AND THEIR CHARACTERISTICS:

- **Cabernet Sauvignon:** Full-bodied wines with a toasty cedar taste.

- **Merlot:** Smooth wines with the flavor of plums.

- **Pinot Noir:** Earthy-tasting wines that evoke the flavor of cherries.

- **Syrah:** Intense, almost meaty flavored wines with a taste of black pepper.

- **Zinfandel:** Fruity, berry-flavored grapes often mixed with green grapes to make rosé wines.

MOST COMMON WHITE GRAPE TYPES AND THEIR CHARACTERISTICS:

- **Chardonnay:** Popular wines with an aroma and taste of tropical fruit.

- **Pinot Grigio:** Crisp, refreshing, dry wines.

- **Riesling:** Sweeter wines with a floral aroma and an undertone of peaches.

- **Sauvignon Blanc:** Citrusy and acidic wines with a grassy flavor.

IDEAL TEMPERATURE FOR SERVING WINE:

- **Red:** 65°F (18°C)
- **White:** 55°F (13°C)
- **Champagne:** 45°F (7°C)

On the rare occasion that you do not finish a bottle of red or white wine, it can be saved. Move the wine to a capped container that will be completely filled with the wine—this removes oxygen, the main spoiling agent. Refrigerate.

BUSINESS
— AND —
PLEASURE

HOW TO ASK FOR A RAISE

The average guy thinks that he deserves more than he's earning. If you feel the same way, here's how to do something about it.

1. **Do your homework.** You should know what others in your field are earning, what you should be earning, and what your employer can afford to pay you. There are a variety of internet resources and professional organizations available to help you understand the salary for your field. Factor in your experience and location with those resources to calculate what you should be earning. Finally, try to determine the financial health of your company, so you'll know if this is a good time to ask for a raise.

2. **Prepare your case.** Combine your research with a detailed report of what you have done for the company during your employment. Highlight key initiatives and the skills you possess that have made you a successful employee. Treat this as if you were interviewing for a job and selling yourself to a prospective employer.

3. **Know the consequences.** What will you do if you don't receive the raise? What if your manager wants to negotiate a bit? Would you consider other benefits in exchange for a salary increase? Prepare for this discussion ahead of time, so you aren't blindsided at the meeting.

4. **Set up an appointment with your manager.** Be sure you are meeting in person. Aim for the end of the day in an office or a quiet conference room.

5. **Present your case.** Express your satisfaction with the company in general, and perhaps outline some of the goals you'd like to accomplish in the near future. Then name the salary that you feel is appropriate for your position and achievements. Consider proposing a number higher than you'd like, so you can negotiate as needed.

HOW TO NEGOTIATE

Whether your goal is a new mattress, a used car, or extra vacation days in a job contract, you need to remember that negotiation is a head game. To be the winner, you must control the situation—and that means being willing to walk away from the deal if you don't get what you want.

1. **Do your homework.** Get competitive pricing. Understand how the deal will work. And know what concessions you can make in your negotiation.

2. **Understand your goal and their goal.** You know what you want to accomplish. What's motivating the other party? Where do they want to end up? If possible, talk to other people in the industry beforehand, so you can gain additional perspective.

3. **Open with an extreme proposal.** Your initial proposal should be far enough away from your goal to allow for you to compromise and still come out a winner.

4. **Listen to the other side** and make small concessions that address their core concerns.

5. **Be prepared to argue.** Research similar products and cite those as examples. Quote prices from other vendors selling or buying the same product. If available, include facts that neither party can dispute. Don't reveal all of your arguments at once.

Instead, use them as examples throughout the conversation.

6. **Be aggressive in your position.** State that you will buy today if the vendor can meet your price. If selling, have the papers ready for signature.

7. **Walk away if you aren't getting anywhere.** Leave your phone number in case the other party reconsiders.

HOW TO GIVE A TOAST

You may be asked to give a toast at a wedding, a retirement party, or a birthday celebration. Use these tips to make the most of the occasion.

1. **Stay sober.** We know you're nervous, but you can drink when it's over.

2. **Keep it short, sweet, and sincere.** Don't force jokes—especially at the expense of the honoree(s). Include several compliments.

3. **Make it personal.** Address the honoree(s) by name. Include your relationship and a few memorable stories or accomplishments.

4. **Own the speech.** Commit the toast to memory, if possible. Speak slowly, clearly, and confidently.

5. **Make a connection with the honoree(s) and the other attendees.** Look people in the eye and raise your glass.

HOW TO MAKE A GREAT FIRST IMPRESSION

You only get one chance to make a first impression. Whether you're meeting your girlfriend's family or a potential client, get it right the first time with these tips.

1. **Look the part.** Dress properly for the setting. When in doubt, overdress.

2. **Greet the person(s) with a firm handshake.** Make eye contact. You can never go wrong with a timeless remark such as, "It's a pleasure to meet you."

3. **Speak carefully and clearly.** Employ a moderate pace that allows you to enunciate. Use proper grammar.

4. **Be polite and courteous in your tone.** Avoid jokes until you are very comfortable with the situation and certain that the joke will be met with the intended response.

5. **Address the person properly and use their name frequently.** In order to do so, it is important to memorize their name upon first introduction.

6. **Focus the conversation on the other person.** Ask questions to learn more about them and to keep the dialogue moving forward.

7. **Listen carefully.** Don't hesitate to use verbal

cues ("I understand") and visual cues (nodding your head in agreement) to indicate that you are paying close attention.

HOW TO GIVE A GOOD COMPLIMENT

It pays to be nice. Always. If this skill doesn't come naturally, follow these simple guidelines.

1. **Be observant and specific.** Your attention to detail will make the compliment more meaningful. Example: "I admire your respect for the environment."

2. **Justify the compliment.** Your reason for giving the compliment will reinforce its sincerity. Example: "I admire your respect for the environment and the way you're taking steps to improve it."

3. **Use an example.** Cement your sincerity by recounting a story. Example: "I admire your respect for the environment and the way you're taking steps to improve it. It was really great how you set up the recycling program at our office."

4. **Ask a question.** This can also act as a conversation starter. Example: "I admire your respect for the environment and the way you're taking steps to improve it. It was really great how you set up the recycling program at our office. Is there anything I can do to help?"

5. **Follow up later.** A thoughtful email or thank-you note is always appreciated. There's no need

to be wordy. It's the thought that counts. Example: "Thank you so much for taking the time to show us how to sort our office recyclables. Your dedication to this project has been inspirational."

HOW TO BUILD A CAMPFIRE

The discovery of fire is one of humanity's greatest accomplishments. Using these instructions, you should have an easier time than our cave-dwelling counterparts.

1. Clear an area at least 10 feet (roughly 3 meters) in diameter. Be sure there is no low-hanging debris nearby. If a fire pit already exists, be sure that all materials, such as tents, clothes, and blankets, are at least 3 feet (1 meter) away from the fire pit.

2. If a fire pit exists, skip ahead to step 3. If not, place rocks or bricks in a circle that is approximately 3–4 feet (1 meter) in diameter.

3. Gather materials. You will need a mixture of kindling, sticks, and larger logs.

   a. **Kindling** is lightweight material that will burn quickly and get the fire started. This could be a mixture of twigs, paper, dry leaves, and/or dry pine needles.

   b. **Sticks** should be a little bulkier and broken to fit inside the fire pit. The sticks should be dead and dry.

   c. **Larger logs** should be dry and able to fit safely inside the fire pit.

4. Place a few handfuls of kindling in the center of the fire pit.

5. Stack the sticks around the kindling in a teepee form. The sticks should lie at a 45-degree angle from the ground, and you should leave room between the sticks to allow oxygen to flow through the teepee.

6. Using the thicker sticks, create a square around the teepee structure. You can do this by placing two sticks on either side of the teepee. Next, stack sticks on the other two sides so that the ends overlap in a log-cabin style. Continue until you are five layers high.

7. Add one or two sticks to the top of the cabin to form a "roof." Do not place too many branches on top of the cabin or you will suffocate the fire.

8. Light a match and place it inside the teepee so that it lights the kindling.

9. If built properly, the kindling will burn and the teepee will ignite the cabin.

10. If the fire needs help spreading, you should encourage it by adding kindling and sticks. You can also fan the fire at the base to help it spread.

11. Fuel the fire with increasingly larger sticks and logs. Remember that larger logs will require sufficient time to heat before burning.

12. When you are finished with the fire, let the fire and logs burn down. Then, pour several buckets of water on the fire (even if it looks like it has extinguished). If it still smokes, shovel some dirt onto the ashes.

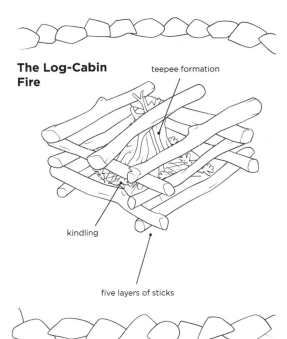

The Log-Cabin Fire

teepee formation

kindling

five layers of sticks

HOW TO CAST A FISHING ROD

Whether you're deep-sea fishing on a special bachelor party weekend or spending a day on a stream with old Pop-Pop, casting a fishing rod is the definitive skill every man should know.

1. Check to ensure you have enough clearance to properly cast the line.

2. Firmly grip the rod near the base with your casting (dominant) hand. The joint attaching the reel to the rod should be between your middle and ring fingers.

3. If you are using an open-faced rod, flip the bail with your other hand while holding the line against the rod with the index finger on your casting hand.

4. With your cast arm in line with the rod, point the rod at your target. Keep the tip raised slightly to eye level.

5. Bending at the elbow, raise your casting hand until the rod is parallel to your body (Figure A).

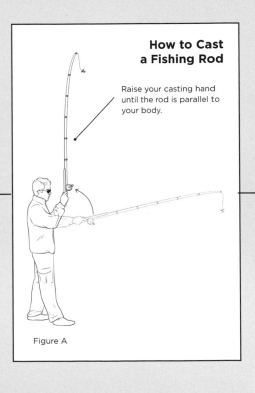

How to Cast a Fishing Rod

Raise your casting hand until the rod is parallel to your body.

Figure A

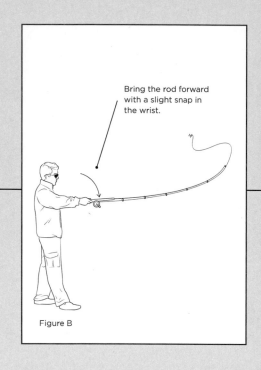

Bring the rod forward
with a slight snap in
the wrist.

Figure B

6. Again, bending at the elbow, bring the rod forward with a slight snap in the wrist (Figure B). When you get about 15 degrees from your starting position, release your index finger's grasp on the line. This will propel the line out into the water.

TIPS:

- Your strength does not affect the length of your cast. It's all in the technique. Many men practice their casting in fields or parks to make the most of their time on the water.

- If you find that you enjoy casting more than fishing, consider enrolling in the International Casting Sport Federation (ICSF), which was founded in 1955 and has member associations in countries around the world.

POKER HIERARCHY AND GLOSSARY

Which ranks higher, a straight or a flush? Before you take your run at the World Series of Poker, it's good to know the answer. Here's the ranking of poker hands in a standard game, from best to worst.

- **Royal Flush:** Ace, king, queen, jack, and ten of the same suit

- **Straight Flush:** Any five cards of the same suit in numerical order

- **Four of a Kind:** Four cards with the same number

- **Full House:** Three cards of the same number and two cards of the same number

- **Flush:** Any five cards of the same suit

- **Straight:** Any five cards in numerical order

- **Three of a Kind:** Three cards with the same number

- **Two Pair:** Two cards with the same number and another two cards with the same number

- **Two of a Kind: Two** cards with the same number

- In all cases, the higher numerical value takes precedence if there is a tie. For example, two aces beat two nines.

Here are some key poker terms that you may hear throughout the course of a game. Obviously, you'll want to understand these terms before you start wagering your hard-earned money.

- **Pot:** The pile of money in the center of the table. It's what you're trying to win.

- **Ante:** A small contribution from each player (before the cards are dealt) to establish the pot. The ante is typically not used in a Texas Hold 'Em–style game.

- **Big blind:** The larger of two forced bets in a Texas Hold 'Em–style game made before the cards are dealt. This is equivalent to a full first-round bet.

- **Flop:** The first three community cards placed face up at the same time in a game of Hold 'Em.

- **No limit:** A version of poker in which a player can bet as much as he'd like when it is his turn to wager.

- **River:** The fifth and final community card placed face up in a game of Hold 'Em.

- **Small blind:** The smaller of the two forced bets in a Hold 'Em–style game made before the cards are dealt. This is typically equivalent to one-third of the full first-round bet.

- **Turn:** The fourth community card placed face up in a game of Hold 'Em.

HOW TO BET ON HORSES

You could walk up to the window and put your hard-earned cash on a horse named "Hard-Earned Cash." But if you want to win real money, follow these simple tips.

1. Pick the right horse(s). The race card will list information about all the horses in the race.

   a. The odds will give you a strong indication of how each horse will fare in that race. Note that 2–1 odds are better than 3–1 odds.

   b. The race card will indicate the last time the horse raced. To ensure that the horse is in racing shape, choose one that has raced within the past month.

   c. The number of horses in the race will give you a sense of the competition. Fewer horses means an easier path to victory.

   d. If the race card shows a C next to the horse's name, the horse has won on this track before. If the race card shows a D, the horse has won at this distance before.

2. Select the dollar amount you'd like to bet. Typically, the minimum you can bet on a horse is $2. The odds indicate the payout multiple for a win. A $2 bet on a horse with 2–1 odds pays $4 plus your original bet of $2. A $2 bet on a horse with 7–1 odds pays $14 plus your original bet of $2.

3. Select the type of bet. The most common types include

   a. **Straight bet to win:** Choose the horse that you think will finish first. ("I'd like ten dollars to win on number five.")

   b. **Straight bet to place:** Choose one horse that you think will finish first or second. ("I'd like ten dollars to place on number five.")

   c. **Straight bet to show:** Choose one horse that you think will finish first, second, or third. ("I'd like ten dollars to show on number five.")

   d. **Exacta bet:** Choose the horses that you think will finish first and second in order. ("I'd like a ten dollar exacta on numbers three and five.")

   e. **Trifecta bet:** Choose the horses that you think will finish first, second, and third in order. ("I'd like a ten dollar trifecta on numbers three, five, and six.")

4. Bring all winning tickets to the cashier after the race. Losing tickets may be discarded.

HOW TO CALCULATE YOUR GOLF HANDICAP

Your golf handicap is the number of strokes you typically shoot over or under par on any given course. Thanks to the handicapping system, you can compete against (and perhaps even beat) first-rate players.

1. Gather the scorecards from your last five rounds. You will need three key pieces of information for each round: your scores, the course ratings, and the slope ratings.

2. For the first round, subtract the course rating from your score. Multiply the result by 113. Then divide this number by the slope rating to determine the differential.

3. Repeat this process for the other four rounds.

4. Multiply your lowest differential by 0.96 to get your handicap. This number will be subtracted from your score at the end of the game to calculate your final score.

FIVE CLASSIC GOLF BETS

If merely playing golf isn't challenging enough for your foursome, here are a couple of wagers designed to keep things interesting.

1. **Nassau:** Each golfer pays $2 to the winner on the front nine, the back nine, and the full eighteen. Select any scoring method you like.

2. **Acey-deucey:** The player with the lowest score (ace) on each hole is paid an agreed-upon amount by each of the other three players. The player with the highest score (deuce) on each hole pays the other three players an agreed-upon amount. If there's a tie (for ace or deuce), there is no payout. This will result in one big winner and one big loser for each hole.

3. **Round robin:** Pair up with a member of your foursome. Declare a winning tandem after six holes and switch your teams. Switch again after the twelfth hole.

4. **Arnies:** This common side bet is paid to any player who scores a par or better without landing his tee shot on the fairway. The round should be played with the intent to land on the fairway.

5. **Putt for dough:** The goal is to 1-putt. Once all balls are on the green, the ball farthest from the pin gets 4 points if the golfer 1-putts. The third farthest

gets 3 points, the second farthest gets 2 points, and the closest gets 1 point. Points are only awarded for 1-putts. Anyone who 3-putts loses 1 point. Anyone who holes out from off the green receives 5 points. Tally the totals at the end of the game and pay out.

LOVE
AND
RELATIONSHIPS

HOW TO MEET SOMEONE IN PERSON

In addition to making friends in adulthood (see page 70), looking for love can be intimidating. Whether it's striking up a conversation on the subway or meeting the person you've been messaging on a dating app, here's how to break the ice with someone new.

1. **Stay calm and confident.** What do you have to lose?

2. **Introduce yourself.** And make sure that you've gotten their name right. If you have trouble with names, connect theirs to a word or image that reminds you of the person.

3. **Ask questions.** Consider topics such as their job, their family, if they have pets, or simply how their day is going. Show this person that you are interested in more than just their looks. Resist the urge to boast. They'll be more impressed if you display an ability to listen and make good conversation.

4. **Be confident but casual.** Maintain eye contact. Have good posture and poise. If their body language is similar to yours, chances are they're interested—but you won't know until you ask! On the other hand, if they seem disinterested, take the hint and move on.

5. **Don't get uptight.** If you find yourself saying something corny, have the good nature to laugh at yourself and the situation.

6. **Ask for their number** and suggest that the two of you get together within the next week. If you suggest plans in person, you'll have something to talk about when you call them later. If they say no, respect their wishes. The rejection may sting for a bit, but don't let it prevent you from striking up another conversation with someone else in the future.

7. **Don't be afraid to call them**, but resist the urge to call or text multiple times a day.

FIVE CONVERSATION STARTERS IN FIVE LANGUAGES

ENGLISH	FRENCH	SPANISH
"Hi. My name is . . ."	"Bonjour. Je m'appelle . . ."	"Hola. Mi nombre es . . ."
"What's your name?"	"Comment tu t'appelles?"	"Cómo te llamas?"
"What do people do for fun around here?"	"Qu'est-ce qu'on fait pour s'éclater ici?"	"Que hace la gente aqui para divertirse?
"May I have the pleasure of this dance?"	"Voulez-vous m'accorder cette danse?"	"Puerdo tener el honor de este baile?"
"Can I buy you a drink?"	"Je peux t'offrir un verre?"	"Puedo invitarte a un trago?"

GERMAN	ITALIAN
"Hallo. Ich bin . . ."	"Ciao. Lo mi chiamo . . ."
"Wie heißt du?"	"Tu come ti chiami?"
"Was macht man hier, wenn man einen draufmachen will?"	"Cosa si fa qui per divertirsi?"
"Darf ich um diesen Tanz bitten?"	"Posso avere l'onore di questo ballo?"
"Kann ich dich zum Drink einladen?"	"Posso offrirti da bere?"

HOW TO LAST TEN MINUTES ON THE DANCE FLOOR

Whether celebrating at a formal reception or spending a night out at the club, you're likely to have more fun if you are a confident dancer. No one's expecting you to move like Fred Astaire. You just need to stick to the basics.

SLOW DANCING:

1. Face your partner.

2. Place both hands on the small of their back. Or place your dominant hand on the small of their back and your other hand stretched away from your body, holding their hand.

3. Slide from side to side while taking small steps forward to move in a clockwise motion. Ideally, your footwork is a mirror image of theirs, and your left foot moves to your left as their right foot moves to their right.

4. Use your dominant hand to gently guide your partner in the direction you want them to move.

5. Maintain eye contact with your partner. At first, you may need to watch your feet to get a handle on their dance style. And you'll want to look around to make sure you don't crash into other couples. But ultimately, you should look straight ahead.

6. Compliment their dancing or make small talk.

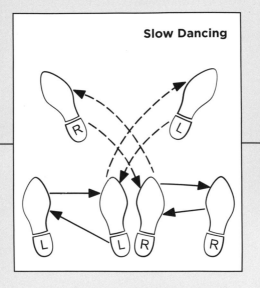

Slow Dancing

FAST DANCING:

1. Soak in the atmosphere. Get a feel for the type of music that is being played and how others are dancing.

2. Listen to the music and find the beat. Bounce your body to get the rhythm.

3. When you're ready, find a place on the dance floor. Circle up if there's a group. Or face your partner.

4. Start with your feet together. Move your right foot to the side and bring it back in. Then do the same with your left foot. Keep going. Mix it up by stepping forward, backward, and diagonally.

5. Move your arms to the beat. Don't flail them around, but don't keep them stiff either.

6. Face forward and try to make it look effortless. You don't want to concentrate too hard.

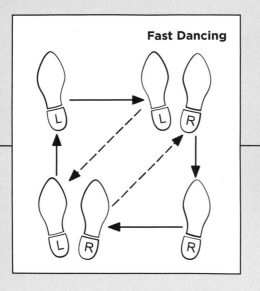

TIPS FOR TAKING A GREAT PHOTOGRAPH

Smartphones have made us all amateur photographers. Here are some tips for capturing group shots and selfies that will help you and your partner or friends remember those magical moments.

1. Read the instruction manual that comes with your camera or smartphone. Familiarize yourself with all of its features. Most contemporary digital cameras and smartphones will do a lot of the work—including lighting and focusing—automatically.

2. To assist in composition, visualize a tic-tac-toe grid over the image in your viewfinder. Then place your subject near one of the corners of the center square. Placing the subject a bit off-center creates a more interesting photograph.

3. Watch your background. Wait for bystanders to get out of the way. Be certain there are no trees or skyscrapers "sticking out" of your subject's head.

4. Check your lighting. If you are outdoors, avoid direct lighting, which may cause squinting and shadows. Also, unless you're photographing a sunset, it's generally better to stand with your back to the sun. If you are indoors, consider turning on more lights or moving lights closer to your subject.

5. Try unique angles. They may bring a whole new perspective to your photograph.

6. Although more difficult to get right, an action shot or candid offers a more realistic shot since the facial expressions will not seem as forced. To ensure good candids, practice by taking lots and lots (and lots) of photographs. Remember, you can always delete the bad ones.

7. When taking a selfie, it's important to find your best angle. Take a bunch of photos with the smartphone in different positions and determine which one you like the best. Also remember to smile confidently but not in a forced way. And push your neck forward to accentuate your jawline and reduce the appearance of a double chin.

HOW TO GIVE A GREAT MASSAGE

A massage is a great way to bring two people together in an intimate moment. When done properly, it relieves stress and channels positive energy. Offer your partner a massage, and if they're in the mood, follow these steps.

1. Set the mood. Eliminate all outside distractions, such as pets and children. Dim the lights. Draw the curtains. Set the room to a comfortable temperature. Play calm and relaxing music.

2. Have your partner disrobe as much as they feel comfortable with. It's possible to give a good massage over clothing, but it's not ideal. Depending on your relationship, you might leave the room during this step.

3. Ask your partner to lie facedown on a firm surface that supports their whole body.

4. You or your partner should drape a plain sheet over their body. During the massage, you will fold back the sheet when you wish to massage a specific area and replace it when you move to another area.

5. Quality massage oil can be the difference between a good massage and a great one. Avoid cheap oils with synthetic scents and greasy textures. Warm the massage oil by rubbing it between your palms.

6. Employ the following basic strokes:

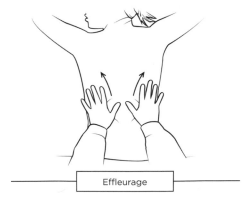

a. **Effleurage:** Apply soft and fluid strokes firmly with the palm of your hand.

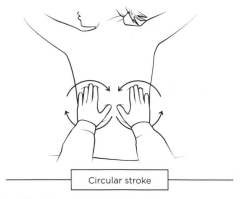

b. **Circular stroke:** Apply pressure as you move your hand in a fluid motion.

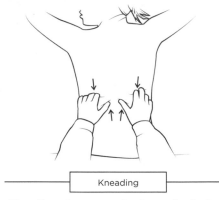

Kneading

c. Kneading: Squeeze and release the flesh and muscle.

7. Begin with their shoulders. Make smooth and soft strokes using your entire hand. Pull the stress away from their core and out of their body.

8. Gently work down to their back. Remember that you are not a licensed chiropractor; go easy and don't apply too much pressure.

9. Work on their arms, hands, and fingers, then move to their legs, feet, and toes. Finish with a scalp rub using only your fingertips.

10. Use a soft towel to wipe the oil away.

Tip: Don't offer a massage with the expectation of anything in return. If your partner is looking for something more sensual, you'll know.

HOW TO HOLD A BABY

Whether you're preparing for fatherhood or just friends with parents of a newborn, you should be comfortable holding a baby. And it's good to know how to do that before you are thrust into the moment. So be prepared and try the simple "cradle hold" (Figure A).

1. Place the baby's head in the crook of your arm (the inside bend of the elbow).

2. Secure the baby's body with that hand.

3. Use your free arm to support the baby's bottom.

4. To calm a fussy baby, rock your arms gently back and forth.

Figure A

And if you really want to show off, hold the baby in the "potato sack" carry (Figure B).

1. Position yourself behind a baby in the facedown position.

2. Slide your dominant hand between the baby's legs, resting it palm up on the baby's chest.

Figure B

3. Use your other hand to secure the baby.

4. Scoop up the baby and carry at your side, as if holding a football.

For older babies who have greater head and neck control, the hip hold is also recommended (Figure C).

1. Rest the baby's bottom on your hip, with their chest resting against your side.

2. Wrap that same arm around the baby's bottom and lower back.

Another option for older babies is to hold them so that they can see what is going on—the "faceout hold" (Figure D).

1. Support the baby's back by placing it against your chest so that the baby is facing forward.

2. Place one arm under the baby's bottom.

3. Place the other arm across the baby's chest.

Figure C

Figure D

HOW TO ENTERTAIN CHILDREN

Engaging with children can be intimidating if it doesn't come to you naturally. But it can also be rewarding for you, fun for them, and—if they're someone else's kids—helpful for their parent. Here are a few ideas to entertain kids at different ages. Always be sure you have the parent's permission before you engage.

TODDLERS

For kids ages 1 to 3 years old, it's important to keep activities simple and lighthearted. With these kids, the onus is more on you to provide the fun.

- **Play with their toys.** Sit with them on the floor. Play with their cars, trains, action figures or dolls. Give a voice to the toy and talk to the child. Start a puppet show with their stuffed animals. Build a tower out of blocks and let them smash it to the ground.

- **Chase them.** Get down on your hands and knees and crawl around making animal noises. Have some fun with it and you'll have them laughing with you.

- **Read a book.** Ask the child or parent for their favorite book, and sit and read to them.

- **Take them for a walk.** For very young kids, this is best done with the child in the stroller. You can point out different things on the walk like trees, birds, and cars. Remember to bring parent-approved snacks if you'll be out for a while.

PRESCHOOLERS

With kids ages 3 to 5 years old, the activity can be a little more involved and a little more active.

- **Make your own cartoon.** Ask the child to draw a hero and a villain on a piece of paper. Together, give them names. Then ask them to tell you a story using those characters. Or, you can tell a story using the characters.

- **Create a scavenger hunt.** You could create a formal list or just give them prompts: *Find something that starts with the letter B.* When the child returns, give another letter. You can add some urgency by having them bring back the item before you count to 10.

- **Play a verbal game.** Take turns naming an animal for each letter of the alphabet.

- **Design a treasure hunt.** Hide a coin somewhere in the room or house. Let them find it. As a bonus, let them keep the coin as a reward.

ELEMENTARY SCHOOL CHILDREN

Kids ages 6 to 11 years will enjoy activities that are more creative and mentally stimulating.

- **Do a craft project.** It could be as simple as painting pine cones or something more elaborate like building a bird feeder. Seek out an age-appropriate craft online and purchase or gather the materials ahead of time. These projects also offer a sense of accomplishment that build a child's confidence.

- **Tell riddles.** Kids love to solve puzzles. Here are a few simple riddles that you can easily memorize.

  ◊ *It belongs to you, but your friends use it more. What is it?* (Your name.)

  ◊ *There's only one word in the dictionary that's spelled wrong. What is it?* (Wrong.)

  ◊ *It has keys, but no locks. It has space, but no room. You can enter, but can't go inside. What am I?* (A keyboard.)

- **Build a story.** Ask the child to tell you a person, place, thing, and number. Then come up with a story using those four words. Make it funny and silly. Next, reverse roles and have the child tell you a story with four words you give to them.

- **Play sidewalk-chalk Pictionary.** Grab chalk and find a sidewalk or driveway. Take turns drawing pictures that the other person has to guess. You can prepare a list of appropriate words ahead of time or come up with them on the fly.

HOW TO HAVE A PRODUCTIVE ARGUMENT WITH YOUR PARTNER

Inevitably, you will disagree with your partner on something. Hopefully it's not too often. When it happens, it's critical that you approach the discussion in a healthy and productive manner in order to communicate properly and find common ground. Here's how to do it.

- **Consider the timing of the conversation.** Let's face it: there's no good time to argue. And certainly, these interactions can happen unexpectedly. But when possible, aim to have the conversation when both of you have enough time to talk and are able to focus. For example, don't bring up a conflict as your partner is leaving for an appointment. If the argument happens unexpectedly, suggest tabling the discussion until a better time. But don't avoid having the conversation completely.

- **Make the goal about reaching a compromise.** Trying to win the argument means your partner loses—which means you both lose. Instead, think about it as you and your partner against the problem—not each other. Figure out where you can budge and what elements are nonnegotiable. That will likely leave a lot of gray area where you can find common ground with your partner.

- **Listen and ask questions.** Hearing your partner's point of view and asking clarifying questions will help move the conversation toward the goal of compromise. Use nonthreatening language like "Help me understand" to gather more information about how your partner is feeling and why.

- **Share your feelings.** Opening up about your thoughts will enable your partner to further understand your position and what's important to you. Avoid complaints like "you always . . . ," which can sound like accusations and put your partner on the defensive. Instead, make requests that rephrase the topic around you: "I'm stressed about not having time to make dinner each night. Would you mind helping me out on some of the nights?"

- **Remain respectful, calm, and on topic.** Avoid yelling, name-calling, and insulting each other. Resist the temptation to let unrelated issues or past arguments creep into the conversation. If you sense that things are getting too tense, suggest taking a break and revisiting the topic at a later time. Cool off, but don't avoid each other completely in the interim.

- **Know how to apologize.** This is someone you care about deeply. And the goal is to maintain a happy, balanced relationship. Different people and arguments may require different types of apologies. Some people want larger gestures, while others just want to know you've heard them and will do better.

HOW TO SELECT A GIFT FOR YOUR PARTNER

Gifts don't have to be expensive to be memorable. The real key is to make it personal and appropriate to the occasion. Follow these tips to help identify a present that will make a lasting impact.

- **Pay attention.** If you are listening, your partner is likely to drop hints intentionally or unintentionally. Maybe it's a passing comment from something seen in a commercial or something more intentional like pointing out a wish list item while running errands together. Make notes of those items when they come up, and revisit that list when it's time to purchase a gift.

- **Think about your partner's interests and passions**. Consider what hobbies or activities your partner is enthusiastic about. Perhaps there's a practical item that can support their participation. This is especially good for a new hobby that they might not have all the necessary equipment yet.

- **Do something together.** The gift doesn't have to be an item. Trying something new or partaking in a favorite activity together can bring you closer. Select something that matches your partner's interests like concert tickets, a wine tasting, or dance classes.

- **Get crafty.** If you are an experienced musician, write a song. If you are a painter, create a piece of art specifically for your partner. You don't have to be an expert to make something memorable. Work within your comfort zone. Even creating a photo album highlighting special moments from your relationship is meaningful.

- **Ask your partner what they want.** If you are struggling for ideas, be straightforward and ask. If you want to still have an element of surprise to the gift, ask for a list of items that you can choose from. Alternatively, you can ask your partner's friends for suggestions.

- **Don't forget the card.** You don't have to be a skilled writer in order to share your feelings or why you chose the gift. Make it personal and romantic, if appropriate.

Remember, you don't need a reason to buy a gift for your partner. Surprise gifts are always appreciated.

HOW TO BUY A DIAMOND

If you plan on making a marriage proposal, you may be in the market for a diamond engagement ring. To ensure that your investment obtains the desired result, follow these tips.

- **Have a very clear understanding of what your partner wants**. The ring selection is often done in consultation with your partner, who may have a specific style in mind. She may want to visit the store with you. She may want a stone that's not a diamond, or a gem that's ethically sourced. She may have a family heirloom that she wants to repurpose. Have the conversation with her ahead of time, or consult a close friend or loved one that knows her wishes.

- **Consider the color.** In the world of diamonds, color is graded on an alphabetical scale ranging from "colorless" (D) to "light yellow" (Z). You want the diamond you choose to have as little color as possible. Note that grades G, H, I, and J are considered "near colorless" and offer an incredible value (these stones only appear to have color when compared to other diamonds).

- **Consider the cut.** This refers to the general way a diamond is cut into facets and determines the way light travels through the stone, which affects its brilliance. Cut isn't really measured in any unit, but you want to avoid a diamond that seems too squat/shallow or too deep.

- **Consider the carat.** This is the weight of a diamond. It has the largest impact on the price. It will ultimately decide how visible the diamond is in the setting and on her finger.

- **Consider the clarity.** This measurement charts the flawlessness of a stone. Clarity is graded on a scale from "flawless" to "included," with varying stages of imperfections along the way. "Very slightly included" and "slightly included" are in the midrange and considered a solid value.

- **Consider the shape**. Round and emerald-cut diamonds are more traditional, but there are many trendier options available. Ask your spouse-to-be what they like. Since you're getting married, you need to familiarize yourself with this question, anyway.

- **Check the authenticity.** Before purchasing, you are entitled to view the diamond's grading report certifying that it has been examined, scrutinized and graded by a team of gemologists. The report should list all of the diamond's key characteristics, as listed above.

HOW TO PROPOSE

If you plan on taking that next big step, you've got to do it right. Here are some basic tips for popping the question.

1. **Have a conversation.** It doesn't have to be formal. But you should be on the same page with respect to marriage and your future together. Make certain that she's ready and wants marriage. Also be sure that your future plans are aligned with respect to children, where you want to live, and other similar life choices you'll need to make together. Obviously, things can change with time, but it's important to communicate about what you both want out of your life together, as well as what kind of proposal your partner wants.

2. **Buy (or get) a ring.** No matter how big or small, an engagement ring will let her know that you're serious about this commitment. (See page 138 for tips on buying a diamond.) Make sure to keep the ring (either in or out of the box) in a safe yet easily accessible place, such as the pocket of your blazer.

3. **Pick a location.** Plan a special romantic evening based on your soon-to-be fiancée's tastes. If she gets easily embarrassed, do not propose in a crowded restaurant or on the JumboTron at a sports stadium. Choose a place that is meaningful for both of you.

4. **Make it personal.** Consider what things might make the proposal more special for your partner. She may want you to kneel. She may want to propose to you. She might want both sets of parents in attendance or available to meet up with afterward. Try to get a sense of what your partner wants as you plan to pop the question.

5. **Express your feelings.** On the big night, tell her how much you love her and how much she means to you. Make eye contact, and don't rush your words. Savor the moment you'll both remember forever.

6. **Offer her the ring.** When you give her the ring, hold it toward the light to make it sparkle. Wait until she has accepted your proposal to put it on her ring finger.

7. **Ask her to marry you.** Always introduce the idea of marriage in the form of a question. That way there is no confusion, and her choice of answers is fairly simple. Wait for her to answer before continuing with the evening. Good luck!

WEDDING ANNIVERSARY CHART

Most guys can remember their wedding anniversary. But can they remember the appropriate gift for each milestone? When in doubt, consult this chart, which might point you toward an appropriate gift. And always add flowers.

YEAR	GIFT	GEM
1	Paper	Gold
2	Cotton	Garnet
3	Leather	Pearls
4	Linen	Blue Topaz
5	Wood	Sapphire
10	Tin	Diamond
15	Crystal	Ruby
25	Silver	Silver
50	Gold	Gold

STUFF YOU SHOULD KNOW BUT I CAN'T TELL YOU

1. Birthdays and anniversaries for your partner, all close family members, friends, and key coworkers

2. How to escape your house during a fire

3. The best bar and restaurant in your neighborhood for visiting out-of-towners

4. Your signature cocktail, so you're never dumbfounded when called upon

5. Your shirt size, pant size, and jacket size

6. Your signature dish, so you're always prepared to impress a date/your partner

7. Your favorite book, movie, and band

8. Your partner's favorite book, movie, and band

9. Your family history, so that you can tell it to your children someday

10. What you want out of life

HOW TO SAY THANK YOU

1. Keep it short and simple.

Thanks to Jason Rekulak for initially encouraging me to step up to write this book. Thanks to Jhanteigh Kupihea, Jane Morley, and Rebecca Gyllenhaal for advising me in the revision process. Thanks to Ryan Hayes for the sweet new cover. And thanks to everyone at Quirk Books for making this book and all of our books the best products on the planet.

Thanks to my family: Randi, Ilivia, Sawyer, Phil, Sheryl, Mandi, Adam, Lexi, Marley, Harvey, Rosalie, Brett, Shawn, Andrew, Ashley, Hailey, Brian, and Teddy.

And thanks to my friends because the journey is made all the better by the people who surround you.